QUOTES

DARREN HENLEY
& TIM LIHOREAU

BOOSEY & HAWKES

London · New York · Berlin · Sydney

Also published by Boosey & Hawkes:
The Classic FM Pocket Book of Music

Published in 2004 by Boosey & Hawkes
Music Publishers Ltd, in association with
Classic FM

INTRODUCTION

Talking about music will never be a substitute for performing or listening to it, but we hope that this collection of great quotes will prove to be the next best thing.

We've arranged the quotes into sections dealing with composers, conductors and musicians. Singers, of course, make up a separate section.

In addition, insults get a section of their own (after all, classical musicians have such a large repertoire of them), as do some of the many barbs directed towards one composer in particular – Wagner.

MUSICAL THEORIES

The story probably went something like this: first came the wheel. Then came the cart. A few moments after that came the backseat driver, who proceeded to commentate from the back of the cart.

From time immemorial, the moment anything vaguely significant happened, there appears to have been someone on hand to theorise, posit and hypothesise.

Here are just a few examples of what some people thought it was all about.

It being music, of course.

I don't know much about classical music. For years I thought the Goldberg Variations were something Mr and Mrs Goldberg tried on their wedding night.

Woody Allen
Film actor and director
Stardust Memories (1980)

Music hath charms to soothe the savage beast, but I'd try a revolver first.

John Billings
Humorist

Learning music by reading about it is like making love by mail.

Isaac Stern
Violinist

Even Bach comes down to the basic suck, blow, suck, suck, blow.

Larry Adler
Harmonica player

Music with dinner is an insult both to the cook and the violinist.

G. K. Chesterton
Writer

Creativity is more than just being different. Anybody can play weird – that's easy. What's hard is to be as simple as Bach. Making the simple awesomely simple, that's creativity.

Charles Mingus
Composer

Definition of a true musician: one who, when he hears a lady singing in the bathtub, he puts his ear to the keyhole.

Morey Amsterdam
Actor and comedian

There's only two ways to sum up music: either it's good or it's bad. If it's good you don't mess about it – you just enjoy it.

Louis Armstrong
Trumpet player

[Music] can be made anywhere, is invisible, and does not smell.

W. H. Auden
Poet
In Praise of Limestone (1951)

*Too many pieces of music
finish too long after the end.*

Igor Stravinsky
Composer

I occasionally play works by contemporary composers, and for two reasons. First, to discourage the composer from writing any more, and secondly to remind myself how much I appreciate Beethoven.

Jascha Heifetz
Violinist

About contemporary music:

Three farts and a raspberry, orchestrated.

Sir John Barbirolli
Conductor

Modern music is as dangerous as cocaine.

Pietro Mascagni
Composer

Music helps not the toothache.

George Herbert
Poet

Why should the devil have all the good tunes?

Rowland Hill
Inventor of the
'Penny Black' stamp

I believe in Bach, the Father, Beethoven, the Son, and Brahms, the Holy Ghost of music.

Hans von Bülow
Conductor and pianist

For changing people's manners and altering their customs there is nothing better than music.

Shu Ching
600 B.C.

*[Music] is the only sensual
pleasure without vice.*

Samuel Johnson
Lexicographer

*Military justice is to justice
what military music is to
music.*

Groucho Marx
Actor and writer

Truly there would be reason to go mad if it were not for music.

Peter Ilyich Tchaikovsky
Composer

To listen is an effort, and just to hear is no merit. A duck hears also.

Igor Stravinsky
Composer

One should try everything once, except incest and folk-dancing.

Arnold Bax
Composer

SETTLING THE SCORE

Musicians. Funny bunch. Granted, in many ways they've given us some of life's sweetest moments.

But ask virtually any of them what they think of their colleagues and, well, sweet almost always turns to sour. Sometimes they comment on the works, but mostly, they comment on the people. Well, why beat about the bush. As they say in the circus – go for the juggler!

So here is a whole section devoted to the musical "put-down".

You have Van Gogh's ear for music.

Billy Wilder
Film director and writer

On Hector Berlioz's *Symphonie Fantastique*:

What a good thing this isn't music.

Gioachino Rossini
Composer

Rossini would have been a great composer if his teacher had spanked him enough on the backside.

Ludwig van Beethoven
Composer

About the composer Hector
Berlioz:

*One ought to wash one's
hands after dealing with one
of his scores.*

Felix Mendelssohn
Composer

I played over the music of that scoundrel Brahms. What a giftless bastard! It annoys me that this self-inflated mediocrity is hailed as genius.

Peter Ilyich Tchaikovsky
Composer

I'm told that Saint-Saëns has informed a delighted public that since the war began he has composed music for the stage, melodies, an elegy and a piece for the trombone. If he'd been making shell-cases instead it might have been all the better for music.

Maurice Ravel
Composer, who himself worked as an ambulance driver during the first world war

Obituary of Jacques Offenbach, the man who composed the *Can-Can*:

He has written nothing that will live, nothing that will make the world better. His name as well as his music will soon be forgotten.

Chicago Tribune

About Claude Debussy's *La Mer*:

The audience . . . expected the ocean, something big, something colossal, but they were served instead with some agitated water in a saucer.

Louis Schneider
Composer

Debussy is like a painter who looks at his canvas to see what more he can take out. Strauss is like a painter who has covered every inch and then takes the paint he has left and throws it at the canvas.

Ernest Bloch
Composer

Listening to the fifth symphony of Ralph Vaughan Williams is like staring at a cow for 45 minutes.

Aaron Copland
Composer

About the composer Nikolai
Rimsky-Korsakoff:

*What a name! It suggests
fierce whiskers stained with
vodka!*

The Musical Courier

At the premiere of Mozart's opera,
The Marriage of Figaro:

*Far too noisy, my dear
Mozart. Far too many notes.*

Emperor Joseph II

To a violinist who believed that a
passage was impossible to play:

*When I composed that, I was
consarious of being inspired
by God Almighty. Do you
think I consider your puny
little fiddle when He speaks
to me?*

Ludwig van Beethoven
Composer

On his way out of a party:

If there is anyone here whom I have not insulted, I beg his pardon.

Johannes Brahms
Composer

COMPOSE YOURSELF

Now this is a revealing section: composers, and what they said about the art of composing. Surprisingly, there's very little of the luvvie in here. Instead, on the whole, the great composers seemed to have two feet very much on the ground.

Read on and you'll find out why Mozart identified with female pigs and what could be called The Rossini Doorstep Challenge – although, as far as we can tell, there is no hard evidence to suggest that Rossini ever took in washing.

*It is clear that the first
specification for a composer
is to be dead.*

Arthur Honegger
Composer
I am a Composer (1951)

We're not worried about writing for posterity. We just want it to sound good right now.

Duke Ellington
Composer

Composers shouldn't think too much – it interferes with their plagiarism.

Howard Dietz
Song writer

A good composer does not imitate; he steals.

Igor Stravinsky
Composer

*Since Mozart's day,
composers have learnt the
art of making music throatily
and palpitatingly sexual.*

Aldous Huxley
Writer

I write as a sow piddles.

Wolfgang Amadeus Mozart
Composer

It is sobering to consider that when Mozart was my age, he had already been dead for a year.

Tom Lehrer
Satirist

The old idea . . . of a composer suddenly having a terrific idea and sitting up all night to write it is nonsense. Night time is for sleeping.

Benjamin Britten
Composer

Composing is like driving down a foggy road toward a house. Slowly, you see more details of the house – the colour of the slates and bricks, the shape of the windows. The notes are the bricks and mortar of the house.

Benjamin Britten
Composer

*In order to compose, all you
need to do is remember a
tune that nobody else has
thought of.*

Robert Schumann
Composer

*Never compose anything
unless not composing it
becomes a positive nuisance
to you.*

Gustav Holst
Composer

*It is not hard to compose, but
it is wonderfully hard to let
the superfluous notes fall
under the table.*

Johannes Brahms
Composer

Give me a laundry list and I will set it to music.

Gioachino Rossini
Composer

*Every composer knows the
anguish and despair
occasioned by forgetting
ideas which one has no time
to write down.*

Hector Berlioz
Composer

Composers tend to assume
that everyone loves music.
Surprisingly enough,
everyone doesn't.

Aaron Copland
Composer

Pay no attention to what the critics say. No statue has ever been put up to a critic.

Jean Sibelius
Composer

*Having adapted Beethoven's
sixth symphony for* Fantasia,
*Walt Disney commented:
"Gee! That'll make
Beethoven".*

Marshall McLuhan
Media commentator
Culture is Our Business (1970)

Beethoven and Liszt have contributed to the advent of long hair.

Louis Moreau Gottschalk
Pianist, composer and conductor

WAGNER

Imagine this: all the composers have met up in the afterlife and a roll-call is being taken of their names. When it comes to Wagner, it turns out that he's the only one who's insisted on a separate room.

He merits his own section not because we think he is the greatest, but because whenever musicians were looking for a target, more of them set their sights on "Little Richard" than any other. Perhaps his mother should have taught her somewhat vertically challenged son, that size isn't everything.

I can't listen to too much Wagner. I start to get the urge to conquer Poland.

Woody Allen
Film director and writer
Manhattan Murder Mystery (1993)

I've been told that Wagner's music is better than it sounds.

Mark Twain
Writer

Wagner has lovely moments but awful quarters of an hour.

Gioachino Rossini
Composer

*I love Wagner, but music I
prefer is that of a cat hung up
by its tail outside a window
and trying to stick to the
panes of glass with its claws.*

Charles Baudelaire
Poet

I like Wagner's music better than any other music. It is so loud that one can talk the whole time without people hearing what one says. That is a great advantage.

Oscar Wilde
Writer
The Picture of Dorian Gray (1891)

One can't judge Wagner's opera Lohengrin *after a first hearing, and I certainly don't intend hearing it a second time.*

Gioachino Rossini
Composer

PASSING THE BATON

It's easy to feel sorry for football managers. When all goes well, the team gets the credit. When all goes badly, it's their fault and they're out.

Conductors are a bit like football managers, only in reverse. When everything goes well in a concert, they are portrayed as demigods, for managing to make seventy people play with one voice. When it goes badly, well, they didn't have a chance with those musicians, did they?

Cue a "baton charge" of venom-fuelled quotes, usually aimed at the orchestra.

There are two golden rules for an orchestra: start together and finish together. The public doesn't give a damn what goes on in between.

Sir Thomas Beecham
Conductor

*I am not interested in having
an orchestra sound like itself.
I want it to sound like the
composer.*

Leonard Bernstein
Conductor and composer

Said to a member of an orchestra:

God tells me how the music should sound, but you stand in the way!

Arturo Toscanini
Conductor

You can chase a Beethoven symphony all your life and not catch up.

André Previn
Conductor

A good conductor ought to be a good chauffeur. The qualities that make the one also make the other. They are concentration, an incessant control of attention, and presence of mind – the conductor only has to add a little sense of music.

Serge Rachmaninoff
Composer

To members of his orchestra, who
were not performing well:

*After I die I shall return to
earth as the doorkeeper of a
bordello, and I won't let one
of you in.*

Arturo Toscanini
Conductor

If anyone has conducted a Beethoven performance, and then doesn't have to go to an osteopath, then there's something wrong.

Sir Simon Rattle
Conductor

*You know why conductors
live so long? Because we
perspire so much.*

Sir John Barbirolli
Conductor

Don't perspire while conducting – only the audience should get warm.

Richard Strauss
Composer

The conductor has the advantage of not seeing the audience.

André Kostelanetz
Conductor

The tuba is certainly the most intestinal of instruments – the very lower bowel of music.

Peter de Vries
Writer
The Glory of the Hummingbird
(1974)

Said to a female cellist:

Madam, you have between your legs an instrument capable of giving pleasure to thousands – and all you can do is scratch it.

Sir Thomas Beecham
Also attributed to fellow conductor,
Arturo Toscanini

Harpists spend 90 per cent of their lives tuning their harps and 10 per cent playing out of tune.

Igor Stravinsky
Composer

Never look at the trombones,
it only encourages them.

Richard Strauss
Composer and conductor

BOWING AND SCRAPING

Have you ever met someone famous and been a little disappointed because you found out that they were smaller than you thought, or that they look older in real life?

Well, a similar thing can happen when you ask yourself the question "I wonder what's going through the musician's head when they are playing Chopin, conducting their own music, or singing at La Scala."

Some of these questions are answered in this section, along with the odd tip on how to be a performer. You might find that you wish you'd never asked.

I know two kinds of audience only – one coughing and one not coughing.

Artur Schnabel
Pianist

I'm a flute player, not a flautist. I don't have a flaut and I've never flauted.

James Galway
Flute player

I never understood the need for a "live" audience. My music, because of its extreme quietude, would be happiest with a dead one.

Igor Stravinsky
Composer

Making music is like making love: the act is always the same, but each time is different.

Artur Rubinstein
Pianist

Advice from one pianist to another:

When a piece gets difficult, make faces.

Artur Schnabel
Pianist

The notes I handle no better than many pianists. But the pauses between the notes – ah, that is where the art resides.

Artur Schnabel
Pianist

It's easy to play any musical instrument: all you have to do is touch the right key at the right time and the instrument will play itself.

Johann Sebastian Bach
Composer

You don't need any brains to listen to music.

Luciano Pavarotti
Tenor

After playing Chopin, I feel as if I had been weeping over sins that I had never committed.

Oscar Wilde
Writer

The music teacher came twice a week to bridge the awful gap between Dorothy and Chopin.

George Ade
Humorist

Mine was the kind of piece in which nobody knew what was going on – including the composer, the conductor and the critics. Consequently I got pretty good notices.

Oscar Levant
Pianist and composer
A Smattering of Ignorance (1940)

I'm not handsome, but when women hear me play, they come crawling to my feet.

Nicolò Paganini
Violinist and composer

I cannot tell you how much I love to play for people. Would you believe it – sometimes when I sit down to practise and there is no one else in the room, I have to stifle an impulse to ring for the elevator man and offer him money to come and hear me.

Artur Rubinstein
Pianist

[Musicians] talk of nothing but money and jobs. Give me businessmen every time. They really are interested in music and art.

Jean Sibelius
Composer

Last night the band played
Beethoven. Beethoven lost.

Anon.

BELTING IT OUT

Why does opera have its own section? To answer that, you have to understand that the opera world has a reputation for being a little inward looking, shall we say.

It is no coincidence that the phrase "prima donna" has come to be associated with bad behaviour.

As the legend goes, a singer will be the one at a party saying, "But less of this talk about *me*. Let's talk about *you* – what do *you* think about *me*?"

Is it true? Judge for yourself.

How wonderful opera would be if there were no singers.

Gioachino Rossini
Composer

Singers have the most marvellous breath control and can kiss for about ten minutes.

Jilly Cooper
Novelist

Opera's when a guy gets stabbed in the back and instead of bleeding he sings.

Ed Gardner
Radio personality

About Wagner's opera *Parsifal*:

The kind of opera that starts at six o'clock and after it has been going three hours you look at your watch and it says 6:20.

David Randolph
Conductor

A review of Verdi's opera *Rigoletto*,
shortly after its premiere:

Rigoletto *lacks melody. This
opera has hardly any chance
of being kept in the
repertoire.*

Gazette Musicale de Paris

*I don't mind what language
an opera is sung in so long
as it is a language I don't
understand.*

Sir Edward Appleton
Physicist

If you think you've hit a false note, sing loud. When in doubt, sing loud.

Robert Merrill
Baritone

I cannot switch my voice. My voice is not like an elevator going up and down.

Maria Callas
Soprano

About a soprano:

If she can strike a low G or F like a death-rattle and high F like the shriek of a little dog when you step on its tail, the house will resound with acclamations.

Hector Berlioz
Composer

*No good opera plot can be
sensible, for people do not
sing when they are feeling
sensible.*

W. H. Auden
Poet

After hearing an opera by another composer:

I like your opera – I think I will set it to music.

Ludwig van Beethoven
Composer

*Most people wouldn't know
music if it came up and bit
them on the ass.*

Frank Zappa
Composer

Another book small enough to keep in your pocket . . .

The Classic FM Pocket Book of Music. It's stuffed full of facts about music, not always entirely objectively expressed ("the bassoon's just like a didgeridoo wearing too much jewellery"). It tackles more than 125 subjects ranging from Beethoven to film music. It answers some long overdue questions along the way ("why are conductors like support tights?"). All this in one tiny book. If it had seams, they'd be bursting.